17 Trilobites

EVERYONE SHOULD KNOW ABOUT

STANTON F. FINK

VOLUME VI OF STANTON'S COLORING BOOKS

Acknowledgments

and Dedication

To my father, in whose books I discovered my first monsters.

To Thomas Hegna, whose friendship and scholarly assistance have been irreplaceably invaluable.

To Sam Gon III, who graciously allows me to continue my silly little dream of one day replacing him as the "Trilobite Kahuna."

To my friends, who helped push me to make this.

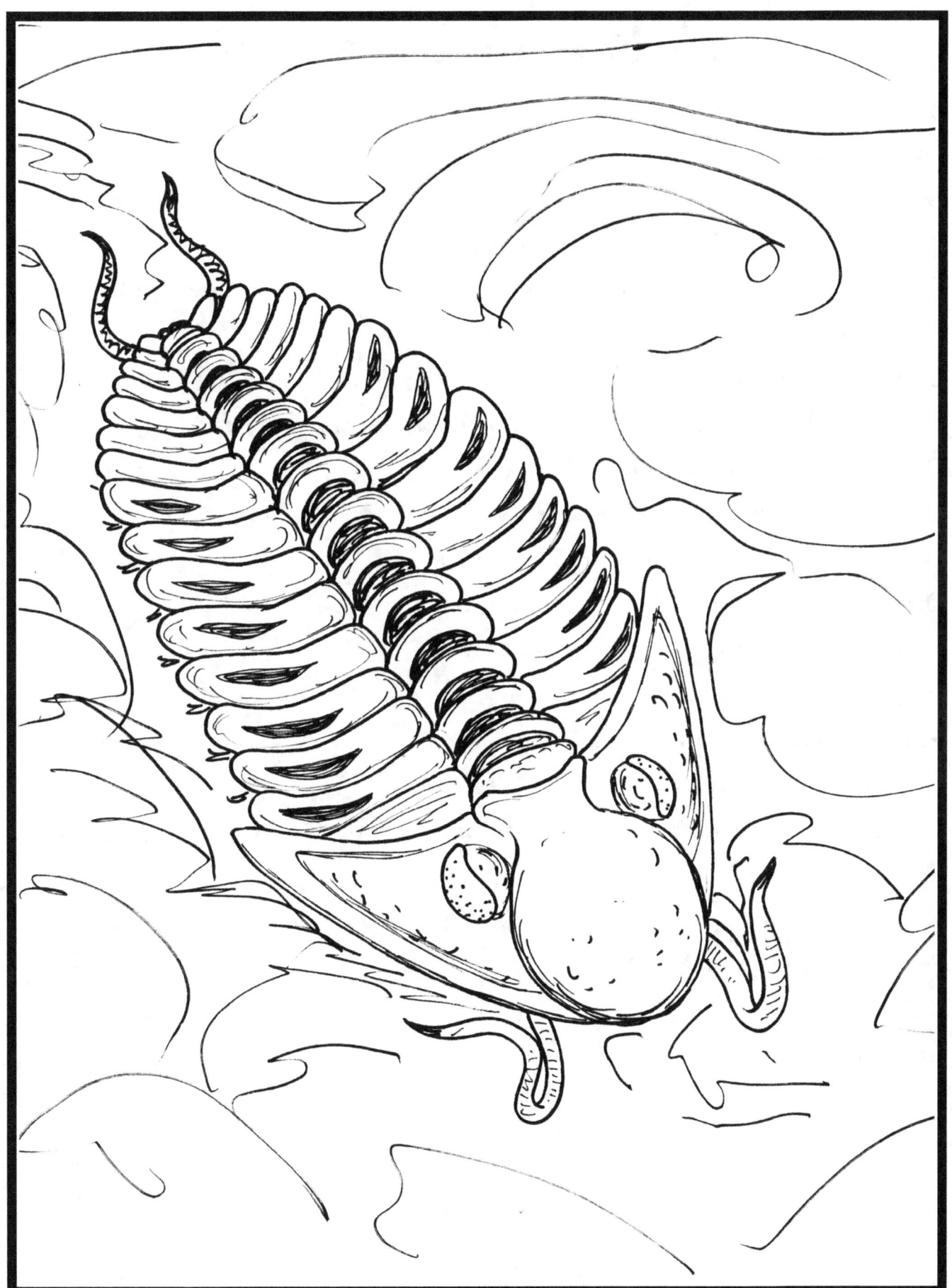

Table of Contents

Introduction

Trilobites are probably the secondmost iconic group of fossil animals after the non-avian dinosaurs. Trilobites lasted about 270 million years, from the Early Cambrian, 521 million years ago, until the end of the Permian 250 million years ago. Although the most primitive known trilobites appear 521 million years ago, that they are already complicated creatures with a worldwide distribution strongly suggests that the ancestral trilobite still remains hidden in the vicissitudes of time and tectonic movements.

During the first half of the Paleozoic, trilobites formed important groups in their respective ecosystems. By the time the Late Devonian Extinction Event came, all trilobites went extinct, save for the Proetids, who continued to persist in marine ecosystems until the very last of them died out by the Permian Triassic Extinction Event.

Humans value trilobites partly for the insights trilobites provide about evolutionary biology in general, and about life in Paleozoic marine environments in particular, and partly for their peculiar, anciently arcane appearances.

Glossary

- **Aquatic**- Living in water.
- **Arthropod**- Any member of the animal phylum Arthropoda, including trilobites, arachnids, crustaceans, insects, myriapods and their relatives. All arthropods have armor-like, jointed exoskeletons made of chitin-derived plates, sometimes reinforced with calcium carbonate, and jointed limbs.
- **Cambrian**- A period of time in the Paleozoic Era from 541 to 485 million years ago.
- **Carboniferous**- A period of time in the Paleozoic Era from 359 to 300 million years ago.
- **Cephalon**- The shield-like structure which formed the head of the trilobite.
- **Chelicerate**- Any member of the arthropod subphylum Chelicerata, and include the arachnids, eurypterids or sea scorpions, and the horseshoe crabs. The chelicerates are thought to be descendants of one of the many minor groups of primitive arthropods from the Cambrian that looked too suspiciously like trilobites, possibly the aglaspids
- **Chordate**- Any member of the animal phylum Chordata, including sea squirts, lancet fish, and vertebrates (such as lampreys, sharks, tuna, frogs, lizards, chickens, and people). All chordates have, at least at some point in their life cycle, a notochord, a long, flexible rod, usually made of cartilage, or, in the case of most vertebrates, cartilage and bone, running down the back from head to tail, directly beneath the neural tube.
- **Devonian**- A period of time in the Paleozoic Era from 414 to 360 million years ago.
- **Ediacaran**- The last period of time in the Precambrian Eon from 635 to 542 million years ago.
- **Fauna**- In an ecological context, "fauna" refers to the animal components of an ecosystem.
- **Formation**- In a geological or paleontological context, a formation is a group of rock layers.
- **Glabellum**- A nose-like, or dome-like structure in the center of the cephalon between the eyes. The glabellum is located above the mouth, and served as a stomach-like storage chamber to hold swallowed food. Plural is "glabella."
- **Mollusk**- Any member of the animal phylum Mollusca, including snails, clams, squid, octopuses, tusk shells and chitons. Most mollusks have a calcium carbonate shell, and a toothed, file-like tongue called a radula. All mollusks have a cape-like organ, the mantle, which usually secretes the shell, and houses breathing organs, and a nervous system.
- **Nekton**- Any aquatic animal that lives either entirely or almost entirely in the water column, and relies on its own swimming or propulsion abilities to keep and move itself in and around the water column. Anchovies, porpoises and ichthyosaurs are examples of nekton.
- **Ordovician**- A period of time in the Paleozoic Era from 484 to 440 million years ago.

- **Paleozoic-** An era of time in the Phanerozoic Eon from 249 to 66 million years ago.
- **Permian-** The last period of time in the Paleozoic Era, the time of "The Great Dying," or most severe of all known extinction events, from 299 to 250 million years ago.
- **Plankton-** An organism that uses water currents and waterflow to as its primary means of transportation in the water column because it is either too small to move long distances by its own power, or lacks the ability to propel itself entirely. Sargassum seaweed and jellyfish are two varieties of plankton.
- **Pygidium-** The last, posteriormost segments of the trilobite which are fused together to form a shield-like structure. Plural is "pygidia."
- **Silurian-** A period of time in the Paleozoic Era from 440 to 419 million years ago.
- **Terrestrial-** Living on land.
- **Thorax-** The central segments which form the body of the trilobite, between the cephalon and the pygidium: most trilobites had an average of nine to eleven thoracic segments, though some dwarf trilobites, such as the agnostids, had as few as two, while some others had as many as twenty. Plural is "thoraces."

Name	# Pakistani Redlich
Species	*Redlichia noeltingi*
Phylum	Arthropoda
Class	Trilobita
Order	Redlichiida
Family	Redlichiidae
Size	Cephalon is 2 to 3 centimeters wide
Time Period	Late Canglangpuian or "Cambrian Stage 4" of the Early Cambrian, about 510 to 509 million years ago
Location	Salt Formation of Western Pakistan
Comments	The Pakistani Redlich, *Redlichia noeltingi,* is the type species of the wide-ranging type genus of the primitive trilobite order Redlichiida. The Pakistani, or Noelting's Redlich is from Early Cambrian-aged marine strata in the Salt Range in Western Pakistan (not to be confused with the Salt Formation in France). Other Redlichs are found in similarly aged marine strata of Southern and Western China, Korea, Iran, Spain, Siberia, Australia and Antarctica.

Redlichiid trilobites are the most anatomically primitive trilobites, and are thought to be ancestral to all other trilobites, except, perhaps, the naraoiids and the agnostids, provided these two groups are eventually unequivocally proven to not be trilobites.

Name	Compact Naraobite
Species	*Naraoia compacta*
Phylum	Arthropoda
Class	? Trilobita
Order	Nektaspida
Family	Nektaspidae
Size	Body length up to 4 centimeters
Time Period	Late Botomian Epoch until Cambrian "Stage 5" of the Cambrian period, from 510 to 507 million years ago
Location	Burgess Shale of British Columbia, Wheeler Shale of Utah, Idaho, and Emu Bay Shale of Australia.
Comments	The Compact Naraobite, *Naraoia compacta*, was originally described by Charles Walcott as a crustacean, under the assumption that it was another "bivalved crustacean." When Harry Whittington dissected a specimen by delicately grinding away the outer layer to reveal legs and external gills identical to those seen in exceptionally preserved trilobite fossils.
	The compact naraobite and other related species are, anatomically, superficially identical to other trilobites, which the main exceptions being that one, the segments on the dorsal side are fused or undifferentiated into few segments, two units in the case of Naraoiidae, and two, the exoskeleton was made primarily of chitin, and not calcium carbonate.
	With the discovery of similar looking arthropods from Early Cambrian China, the idea that the Naraobites and other members of Nektaspida are trilobites has been called into doubt, leading some researchers to postulate that Nektaspida either represents a transition between trilobites and more derived chelicerates (horseshoe crabs, sea spiders, arachnids, etc), or that the nektaspids and trilobites both share similar features that both groups inherited from the as of yet identifed ancestral arthropod. The compact naraobite's lifestyle has been fairly easy to divine, as it appears to be a crawler that ate whatever it could grind up with its spiny legs. Many specimens with healed injuries suggest it was preyed on, possibly by anomalocaridid arthropods.

# Name	# Pea Agnostid
Species	*Agnostus pisiformis*
Phylum	Arthropoda
Class	? Trilobita
Order	Agnostida
Family	Agnostidae
Size	4 to 10 millimeters in length
Time Period	Start of the Late Cambrian, about 492 to 490 million years ago
Location	"*Agnostus pisiformis*" layer of the Alum Shale, Adrarum, Sweden
Comments	The Pea Agnostid, *Agnostus pisiformis*, is a mysterious trilobite known from numerous, often disarticulated fossils from Late Cambrian Sweden. It is "mysterious" in that, even though we know what it looked like, from young juveniles to the pea-shaped adults, many mysteries continue to surround it, from whether or not it extended its body in life, or lived with its body folded like a pair of castanets, to whether or not it and the rest of Agnostida were trilobites, possibly descended from Ptychopariida, or primitive crustaceans.

The lifestyle of the pea agnostid is also mysterious, though, the fact that the fossils often form cobblestone pavement-like breccias strongly suggests the species traveled in large swarm-like groups. Because the pea agnostid had no eyes, and does not have an obviously hydrodynamic physique, many researchers doubt it was pelagic, though, the global distribution of agnostids in general is a thorn in this particular doubt. Other agnostids are suggested to be carnivorous or scavenging benthic dwellers based on how their fossils are sometimes found *inside* of larger trilobites.

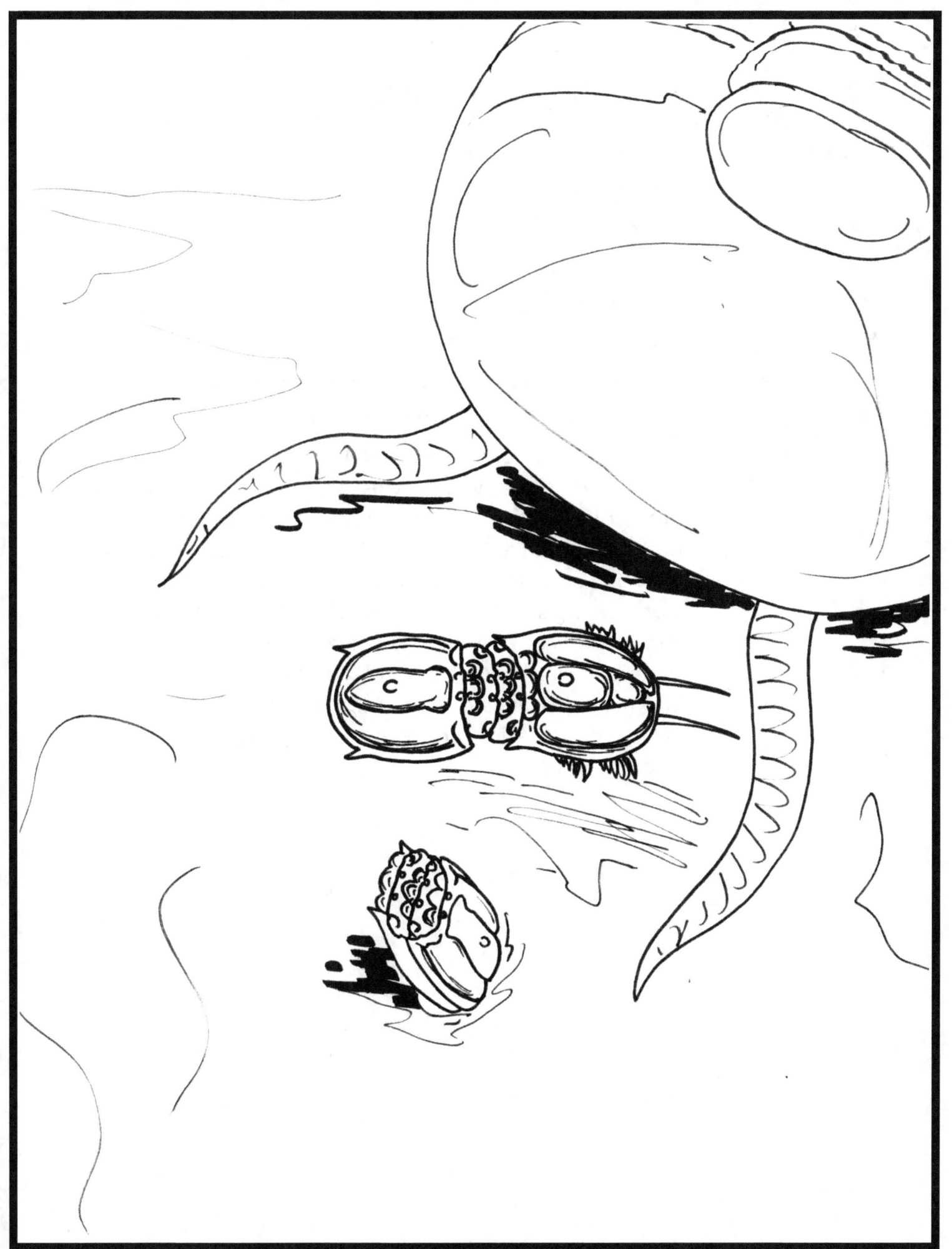

Name	Swedish Helmetrilobite
Species	*Corynexochus spinulosus*
Phylum	Arthropoda
Class	Trilobita
Order	Corynexochida
Family	Corynexochidae
Size	Maybe 2 to 3 centimeters in length
Time Period	Middle Cambrian, about 510 million years ago
Location	Andarum Limestone Formation of Sweden
Comments	The Swedish, or Spined Helmetrilobite, *Corynexochus spinulosus*, is the type species of Corynexochida, a diverse group of trilobites first appearing in the Cambrian and dying out in the Middle Devonian. The Swedish helmetrilobite is a member of a Middle Cambrian-aged corynexochid genus, *Corynexochus*, whose numerous species are found marine strata in what are now western Europe, eastern North America, Asia, and Queensland, Australia.
	The helmetrilobites of *Corynexochus* are poorly studied, as all of the species are known only from disarticulated fragments.

Name

Shandong Swallowstone Trilobite

Species	*Neodrepanura premesnili*
Phylum	Arthropoda
Class	Trilobita
Order	Odontopleurida
Family	Dunkleosteidae
Size	Around 6 centimeters in length
Time Period	Guzhangian Epoch of the Late Cambrian, 501 to 497 million years ago
Location	Kushan Formation of Shandong Province, China
Comments	The Shandong Swallowstone Trilobite, *Neodrepanura premesnili,* is the best known of all swallowstone trilobites of the genus *Neodrepanura,* a genus of odontopleurid trilobites of the family Damesellidae.

The pygidia of many Chinese trilobites are called "swallow stones," 燕子石 (yanzi shi), or "bat stones," 蝙蝠石 (bianfu shi), named so for their resemblance to a swallow or a bat in flight. Swallow and bat stones have been in Chinese culture as good luck charms and as herbal medicine for centuries. The Shandong swallowstone trilobite is the first of the swallowstone trilobites studied by Europeans, being first described as *"Drepanura" premesnili* in 1899. However, even though the Shandong swallowstone trilobite has been known, sort of, to the Chinese for thousands of years, and to the Europeans for over 110 years, the first intact specimen was only discovered in 2011. Other recent discoveries about the Shandong swallowstone include an examination of the hyponome (shown here in the lower right corner), which is a mouthguard-like plate, the size and proportions of which suggests a carnivorous diet.

# Name	# Groovy Foldcheek
Species	*Ptychoparia striata*
Phylum	Arthropoda
Class	Trilobita
Order	Ptychopariida
Family	Ptychopariidae
Size	3 to 8 centimeters in length
Time Period	Middle Cambrian, about 513 to 499 million years ago
Location	Skryje-Týřovice area and the Jince Formation of Bohemia, Czech Republic
Comments	The Groovy Foldcheek, *Ptychoparia striata*, is one of several trilobites studied by the eminent French paleontologist and 2nd favorite adopted son of Prague, Joachim Barrande. Because of the similarities of the Foldcheek with other related ptychopariid trilobites, the number of species in *Ptychoparia* once ranged into the several dozens. More thorough re-examinations, especially of intact, superbly preserved specimens lead scientists to identify new, distinct species: now, *Ptychoparia* includes only five, or so species found in Middle Cambrian-aged marine strata of the Czech Republic, Pakistan, South Korea, and North America.
	In life, the groovy foldcheek was a bottom-dweller, and probably grubbed about for edible detritus.

Name	Indistinctobite
Species	*Asaphus expansus*
Phylum	Arthropoda
Class	Trilobita
Order	Asaphida
Family	Asaphidae
Size	Up to 6 centimeters long
Time Period	From the upper Floian to Darwillian Epochs, about 475 to 458 million years ago, of the Early to Middle Ordovician Period
Location	Sweden, Estonia and Russia near Saint Petersburg
Comments	The Indistinctobite, *Asaphus expansus*, is one of a complex lineage of asaphid trilobites that lived in an Early to Middle Ordovician-aged muddy, shallow sea in what is now the coastline of the Baltic Sea.

The indistinctobite's genus name comes from a Greek word, ασαφής ("asafis"), meaning "vague," and refers to the ambiguous, pillbug-like appearance similar to numerous other related and unrelated trilobites.

The indistinctobite was a benthic mud-grubber that probably hunted worms and other burrowing invertebrates.

Name	Mustachesleigh
Species	*Hypodicranotus striatulus*
Phylum	Arthropoda
Class	Trilobita
Order	Asaphida
Family	Remopleuridae
Size	Up to 3 centimeters
Time Period	Middle Ordovician
Location	Rust Formation of the Trenton Group, New York State, United States, and Ontario, Canada
Comments	The Mustachesleigh, *Hypodicranotus striatulus*, is a pelagic asaphid trilobite from the Middle Ordovician of what is now New York State and Ontario province. It is thought to be pelagic because of its flattened, submarine-like body, and because of how the way its enormous hypostome covered the underside of its body would have allowed better waterflow while blatantly interfering with a crawling lifestyle on the bottom.
	As with most pelagic trilobites, the mustachesleigh is thought to have been a planktivore.

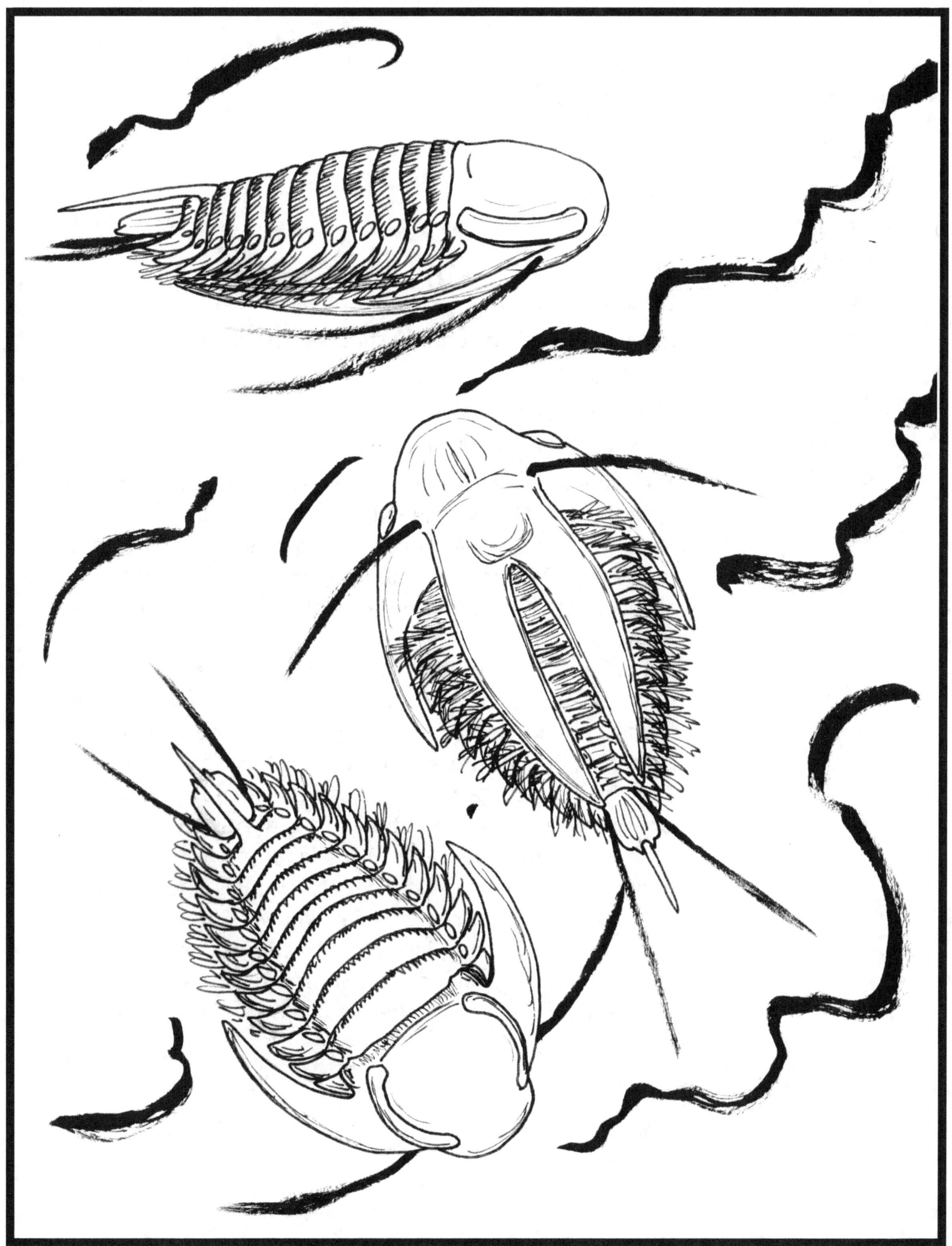

Name	Fringed Lichobite
Species	*Lichas laciniatus*
Phylum	Arthropoda
Class	Trilobita
Order	Lichida
Family	Lichidae
Size	Known from fragments, estimated bodylength maybe 5 centimeters
Time Period	Late Ordovician
Location	Baltic coast of Sweden
Comments	The lichobites of the genus *Lichas* are found in marine strata from the Late Ordovician until the Middle Silurian of Europe, North America, and Morocco. The genus, together with the family and the order, is named after either a Spartan who allegedly discovered the remains of Orestes, or a servant of Heracles.

Lichobites, or lichids, are closely related to the odontopleurids, and some experts group the latter into the former, noting how the two groups diverged during late Cambrian, but still preserved several anatomical similarities.

The Fringed Lichobite, *L. laciniatus*, is known from Late Ordovician-aged marine strata from the Swedish coast of what is now the Baltic Sea. Thus far, it is only known from fragments, though, other species, such as the Moroccan lichobite, *L. marocanus*, are known from complete specimens. Lichobites, including the fringed, are thought to have all crawled along the substrate and gobbled up whatever smaller animals they could find and catch.

Name   Oval Toothriblobite

Species	*Odontopleura ovata*
Phylum	Arthropoda
Class	Trilobita
Order	Odontopleurida
Family	Odontopleuridae
Size	Up to 3 centimeters long, not including spines.
Time Period	Wenloch Epoch of the Middle Silurian, about 425 million years ago
Location	Liteň Formation in Loděnice, Czech Republic, and Gotland, of Sweden.

Comments

The Oval Toothriblobite, *Odontopleura ovata*, is the type species of the order Odontopleurida, and embodies the odontopleurids' reputation for grandiose spinosity among trilobites. The genus name literally translates as "teeth-ribs," can either refer to the way the spines come off of the pleura or segments like fangs, or how the arrangement of spines make the animal look like the horrible jaw of a monster with rib-like teeth.

The original purpose of the odontopleurids' exaggerated spininess is a popular subject of speculation in evolutionary biology. The most obvious conclusion is that the spines detered bigmouthed gnathostome vertebrate predators from swallowing or biting their odontopleurid owners. While this is a reasonable deduction for Silurian and Devonian odontopleurids, it falls apart when one realizes that the odontopleurids evolved their extravagent armament during the Ordovician, before the advent of gnathostomes. Other ideas suggested include spreading the weight of the animal in order to prevent it from sinking into mud, or allow encrusting organisms to grow on them in order to better disguise themselves.

The oval toothriblobite is known from Bohemia and Gotland.

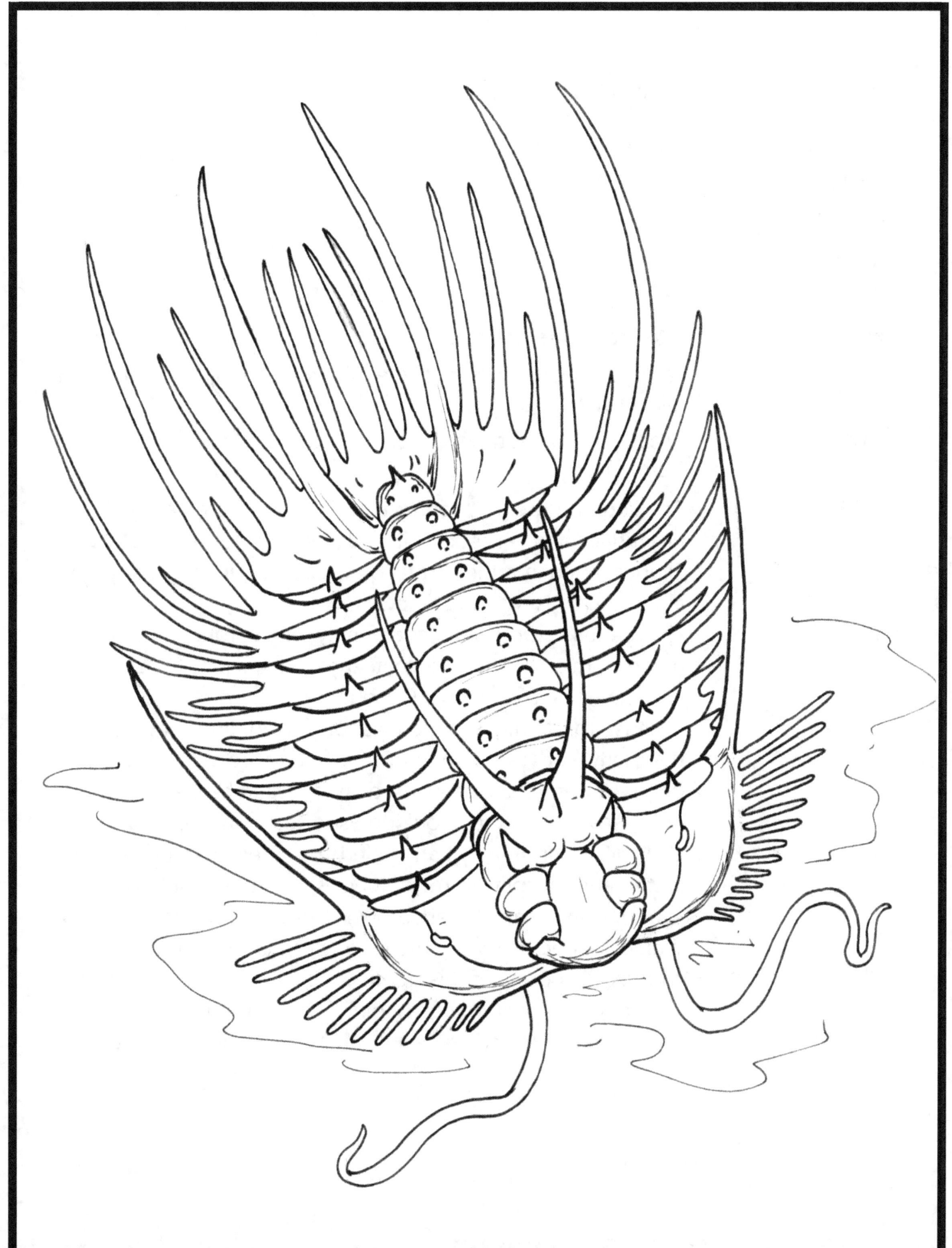

Name	Superb Proetid
Species	*Proetus concinnus*
Phylum	Arthropod
Class	Trilobita
Order	Proetida
Family	Proetidae
Size	1 to 2 centimeters long
Time Period	Late Wenlock Epoch, of the Middle Silurian, 430 to 428 million years ago
Location	Great Britain, Estonia, Island of Gotland in Sweden, and Germany.
Comments	The Superb Proetid, *Proetus concinnus*, is the type species of Proetidae and Proetida: its fossils are found in Middle Silurian-aged marine strata of Great Britain, Germany and along the coast of the Baltic Sea.

The Superb Proetid, *Proetus concinnus*, is the type species of Proetidae and Proetida: its fossils are found in Middle Silurian-aged marine strata of Great Britain, Germany and along the coast of the Baltic Sea.

The genus, along with the family and order, borrows its name from a mythical king of Argos in Ancient Greece, who was the uncle of the hero Perseus.

Because the family Proetidae is long-lived, and that many of the many bodyplans seen in that family are very similar, the genus *Proetus* has been used as a "wastebasket taxon," to hold several similar looking species ranging from the Ordovician until the Carboniferous. Recent studies have systematically split off most species of *Proetus* until only the superb, and the broad-browed proetid, *P. latifrons*, of Wenlock-aged Great Britain and Ireland, are the only confirmed species of this genus.

The animals swimming behind the superb proetid are thylacocephalan crustaceans of the species *Ainiktozoon loganense*.

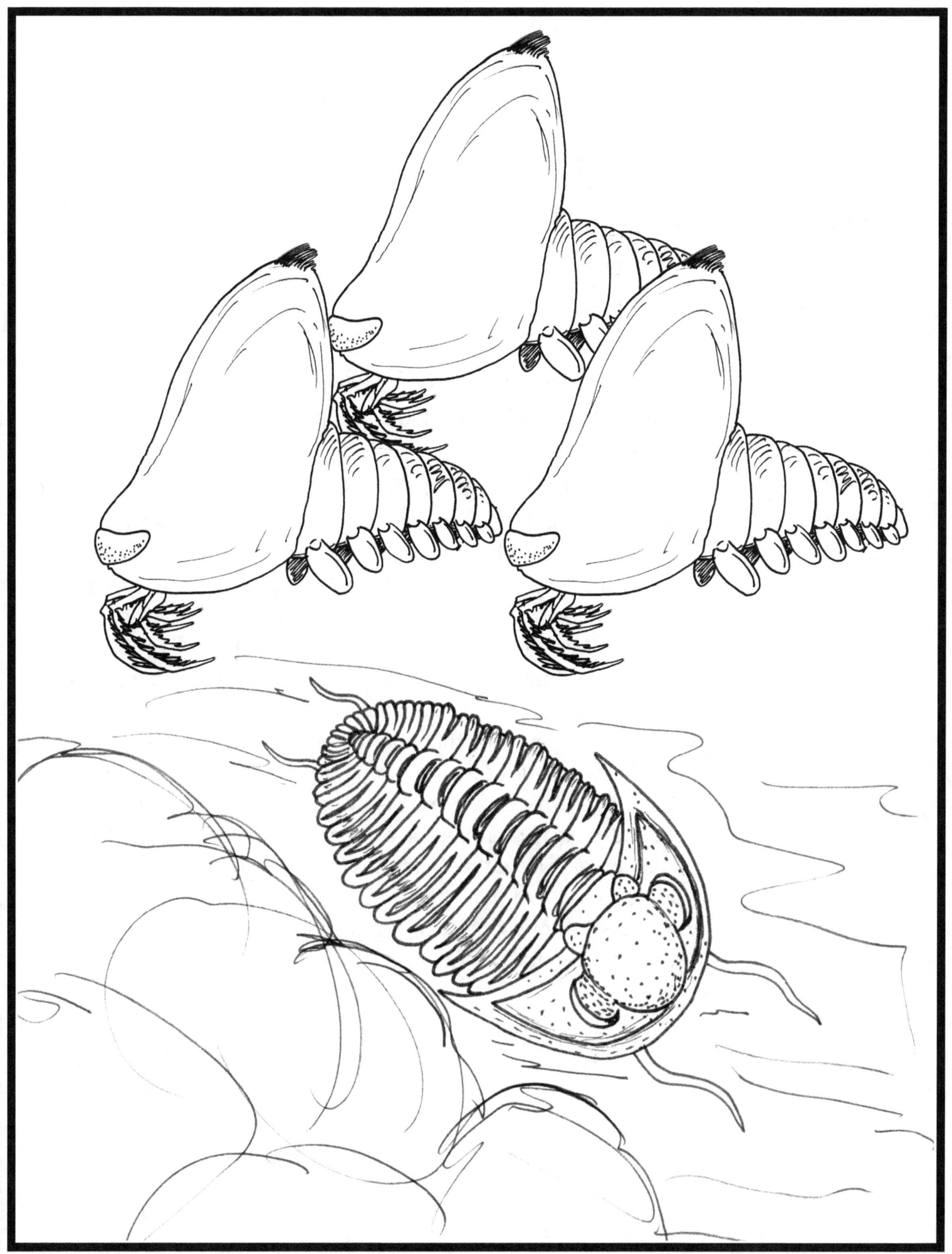

Name	Broad-browed Wartface
Species	*Phacops latifrons*
Phylum	Arthropoda
Class	Trilobita
Order	Phacopida
Suborder	Phacopina
Family	Phacopidae
Size	Average length about 3 to 5 centimeters
Time Period	Eifelian Epoch of the Middle Devonian Period, 397 to 393 million years ago
Location	The Ardennes Mountains, France
Comments	Wartface trilobites are any species of the enormous, Devonian-aged phacopid genus *Phacops,* whose fossils are found in Early to Middle Devonian-aged marine strata in eastern North America, Europe, Northwestern Africa and China. Wartface trilobites, as with all other phacopids of Phacopina that had eyes, have "schizochroal" compound eyes, in that component eye had its own distinct cornea.

There are several, thoroughly documented lineages of wartfaces throughout the world during the first half of the Devonian. The broad-browed wartface, in particular, is the second-to-last member of a French lineage that lived in a shallow sea where the Ardennes Mountains stand now.

Some fossils of wartfaces still have traces of pigments arranged in rows of spots, suggesting that the living animals were spotted for camouflage

Name	## Monstrous Lichobite
Species	*Terataspis grandis*
Phylum	Arthropoda
Class	Trilobita
Order	Lichida
Family	Lichidae
Size	Unknown, fragments suggest an animal up to 60 centimeters long.
Time Period	End of the Emsian Epoch, Early Devonian, about 397 million years ago
Location	Schoharie-Bois Formation, Tri-State Area, New York, United States, and Ontario, Canada.
Comments	The Monstrous Lichobite, *Terataspis grandis*, is the third largest known trilobite. Although it is currently only known from fragments of molted exoskeleton, enough pieces, and intact specimens of relatives, enough material is known to confidently estimate an average adult length of around 60 centimeters.

So far, the monstrous lichobite is dwarfed only by its relative, the Uralichobite, *Uralichas sp*, which is an average of 66 centimeters, and the King Pillbug Asaphid, *Isotelus rex*, which is up to a whopping 77 centimeters in average length. The monstrous lichobite was probably a detritivore, but, given its enormous size and large glabellum, it was probably also an opportunistic predator that ate whatever smaller animal it could dig up, including worms, molluscs, and, smaller arthropods. Whether it could have eaten trilobites like the frog wartfaces, *Phacops rana*, shown here with it, is currently unknown, however.

Name	Giant-Helmeted Swordcolander
Species	*Harpes macrocephalus*
Phylum	Arthropoda
Class	Trilobita
Order	Harpetida
Family	Harpetidae
Size	About 4 centimeters long.
Time Period	Eifelian Epoch of the Middle Devonian, 398 - 392 million years ago
Location	"Pelm-Salmer Weg" at Gees, near Gerolstein of the Rhine Valley, Germany
Comments	The Giant-Helmeted Swordcolander, *Harpes macrocephalus*, is a member of a small, but peculiar order of enormous-cephaloned, medallion-like trilobites called Harpetida. The genus and the order are named after a curved or sickle-like sword from Greek Mythology called a "harpe" (ἅρπη), with the implication that the brim extended from the cephalon appeared to be like a sword blade curved around the head.

The Harpetids diverged from Ptychopariida during the Late Cambrian, and by the start of the Ordovician, harpetids of the family Harpetidae, i.e., the swordcolanders, developed special pits in their cephalon brim that either were the seats of sensory organs, or were holes to allow edible particles through.

The giant-helmeted swordcolander's fossils are found at the "Pelm-Salmer Weg" site at the town of Gees, which, for almost two hundred years, has been mined for beautifully preserved Eifelian-aged trilobites, though, today, collecting at this site has been forbidden since the 1980's ever since collectors used heavy machinery tear up the countryside.

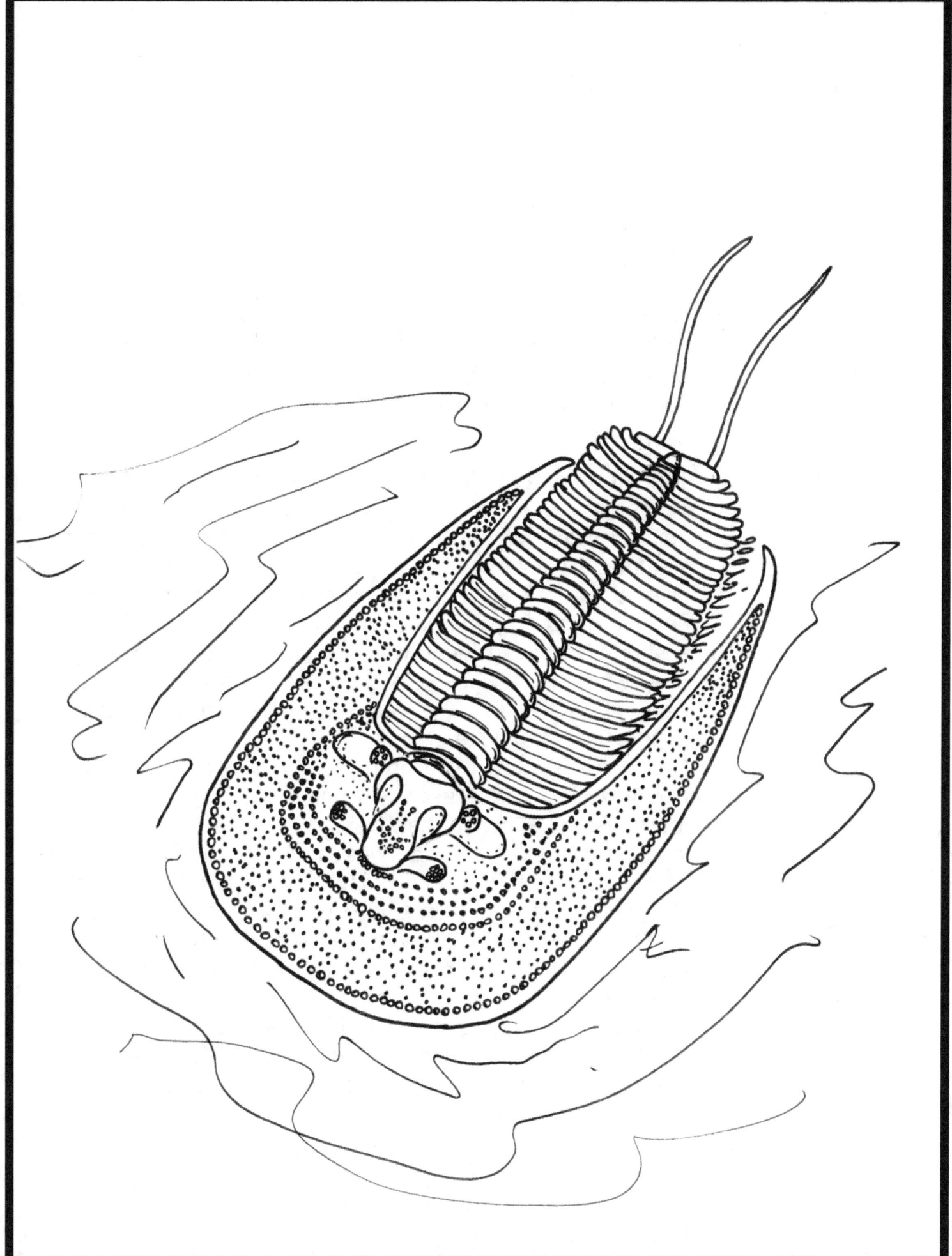

Name	Tridentibites
Species	*Walliserops sp.*
Phylum	Arthropoda
Class	Trilobita
Order	Phacopida
Family	Acastidae
Size	Average bodylength without trident about 3 centimeters
Time Period	Upper Emsian Epoch to the Lower Eifelian Epoch, of the Early to Middle Devonian.
Location	Morocco
Comments	The story of the Tridentibites, or "Trident Trilobites" of *Walliserops* is a weird and sordid tale, from us, humans' point of view. When the first tridentibite species (the long-stemmed tridentibite, *W. trifurcatus*, the lower three in this picture) was described, the purpose of its trident was a peculiar mystery. When a second variety of tridentibite with a short-stemmed trident was found (i.e., the upper right one, which is now described as *W. tridens*), researchers were all "Hooray! The first blatant example of sexual dimorphism in trilobites!"

Of course, very few things in paleontology are rarely ever so blatantly clear-cut, especially when a third variety, then a fourth variety, showing that, instead of one species with two lengths of tridents, there was a cluster of at least six species, each with its own distinct trident (like, for example, the spork, or Lindoe's tridentibite, *W. lindoei*). Aside from helping individuals identify which species other individual tridentibites belonged to, the primary function of the trident continues to elude researchers.

Further compounding this weirdness is the fact that, with the long-stemmed tridentibite, individuals often had forks that bent assymetrically to one side: the reason for this, too, eludes researchers.

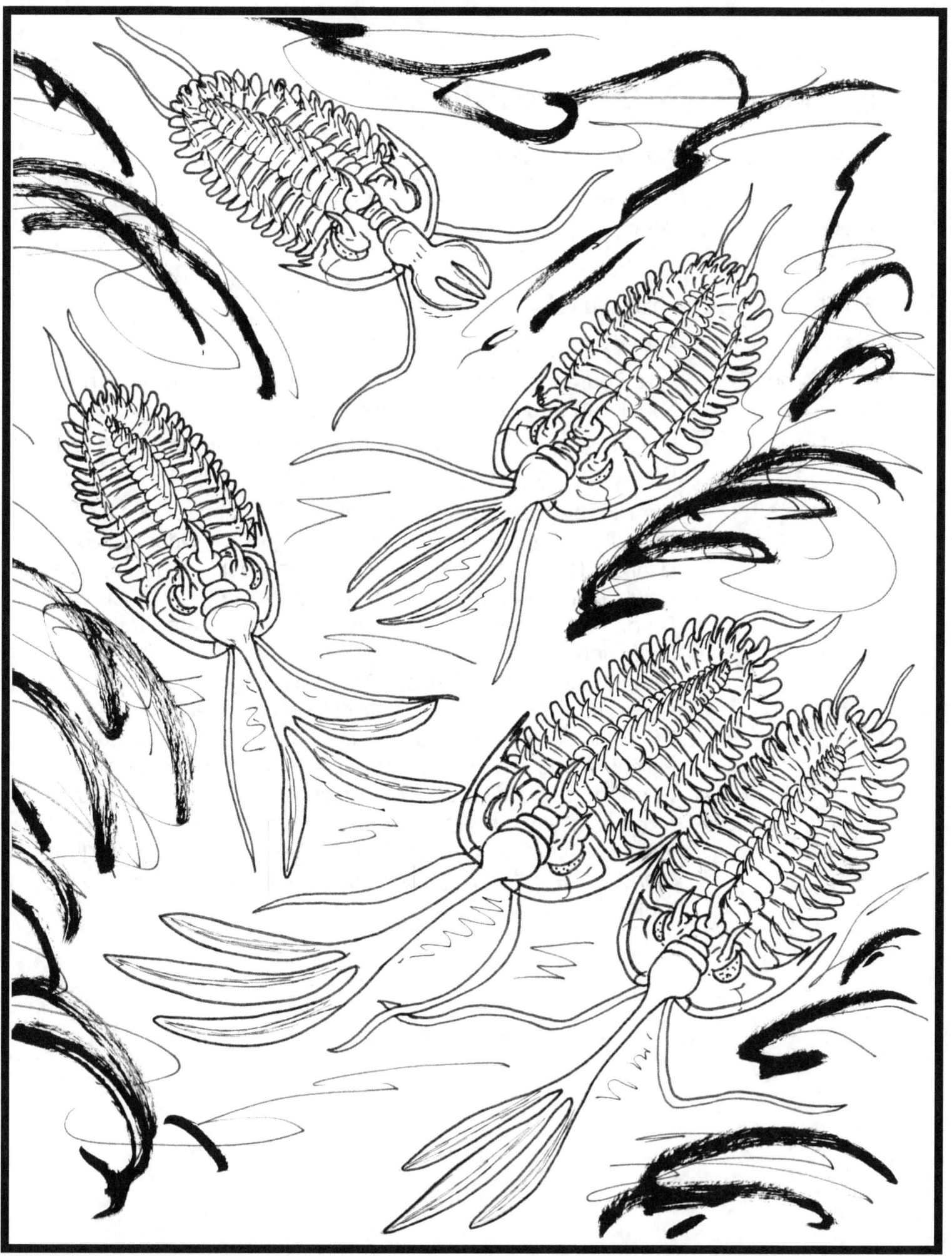

Name — Malchi Creek Proetid

Species	*Malchi magnificus*
Phylum	Arthropoda
Class	Trilobita
Order	Proetida
Family	Phillipsiidae
Size	About 2 to 4 centimeters long.
Time Period	Late Tournaisian Epoch of the Lower Carboniferous Period, about 346 to 345 million years ago.
Location	Malchi Formation of the Rockhampton Group at Malchi Creek, west of Rockhampton, Queensland, Australia
Comments	During the Late Devonian, trilobites began a decline in diversity, with the various Devonian groups, Odontopleura, Lichiida, Harpetida, Corynexochida, Phacopida, and Proetida slowly dying out, one by one, until only the Proetids survive beyond the Hangenberg Event of the Late Devonian Extinction.

During the Carboniferous, the surviving proetids began slowly rediversifying. The Malchi Creek Proetid, or simply, the Magnificent Proetid, *Malchi magnificus*, named for Malchi Creek, where the first fossil specimens were found, was a part of a diversity of Eastern Australian trilobites that arose soon after the end of the Devonian. Here, the larger Malchi is compared with (John) Gibson's Planar Casque, *Planokaskia gibsoni* (which is actually from New South Wales).

Name	Yanagisawa's Paladin
Species	*Endops yanagisawai*
Phylum	Arthropoda
Class	Trilobita
Order	Proetida
Family	Phillipsiidae
Size	Around 3 to 4 centimeters
Time Period	Late Capitanian Epoch, Middle Permian Period about 260 million years ago.
Location	Takakura Formation, Abukuma Mountains, Fukushima Prefecture, Honshu Island, Japan
Comments	During the Permian Period, in the twilight of the trilobites, there were still localities where trilobites remained or became diverse in species, such as in Texas, Oman, China, and in the case of Yanagisawa's Paladin, *Endops yanagisamai*, Japan.
	In Permian Japan, there were several species of proetids from the families Proetidae, Phillipsiidae, and Brachymetopidae: most of these species were of worldwide distribution. Yanagisawa's paladin was endemic, but, the ironically named genus *Nipponaspis* (meaning "Japan's shield") had several species found in Permian China as well as a species in Japan that coexisted with Yanagisawa's paladin.

Bibliography

- Bergström, J.; Hou, X.G.; Hålenius, U. (2007). "Gut contents and feeding in the Cambrian arthropod Naraoia". *GFF*. **129** (2): 71.
- Calner, Mikael, et al. "The first record of Odontopleura ovata (Trilobita) from Scandinavia: part of a middle Silurian intercontinental shelly benthos mass occurrence." GFF 128.1 (2006): 33-37.
- Chatterton, Brian DE, and Stacey Gibb. "Latest Early to Early Middle Devonian Trilobites from the Erbenochile Bed, Jbel Issoumour, Southeastern Morocco." *Journal of Paleontology* 84.6 (2010): 1188-1205.
- Chen, J.-Y., G.D. Edgecombe and L. Ramskjöld. Morphological and ecological disparity in naraoiids (Arthropoda) from the Early Cambrian Chengjiang Fauna, China. Records of the Australian Museum 49(1), pp. 1-24. 1997
- Ebach, M. C., and K. J. McNamara. "A systematic revision of the family Harpetidae (Trilobita)." *RECORDS-WESTERN AUSTRALIAN MUSEUM* 21.3 (2002): 235-268.
- Endo and Matsumoto. 小泉斉. "阿武隈山地・高倉山層群 (ペルム紀) の Phillipsiidae 新属 三葉土." 地球科學 26.1 (1972): 19-25.
- Engel, B. A., and N. Morris. "Ditomopyginae (Trilobita) from the Lower Carboniferous of eastern Australia (i) Australokaskia (Australokaskia), Planokaskia, Malchi n. gen." *Geologica et Palaeontologica* 28 (1994): 79-101.
- KORDULE, VRATISLAV. "Ptychopariid trilobites in the Middle Cambrian of Central Bohemia (taxonomy, biostratigraphy, synecology)." *Bulletin of Geosciences* 81.4 (2006): 277-304.
- Lieberman, B.S. (1994). "Evolution of the trilobite subfamily Proetinae Salter, 1864, and the origin, diversification, evolutionary affinity, and extinction of the Middle Devonian Proetic fauna of Eastern North America". Bulletin of the American Museum of Natural History. 223: 1–176.
- Liu, Qing, and Qianping Lei. "First known complete specimen of Neodrepanura (Trilobita: Damesellidae) from the Cambrian Kushan Formation, Shandong, China." *Alcheringa: An Australasian Journal of Palaeontology* 35.3 (2011): 397-403.
- Ludvigsen, Rolf, and Brian DE Chatterton. "The peculiar Ordovician trilobite Hypodicranotus from the Whittaker Formation, District of Mackenzie." *Canadian Journal of Earth Sciences* 28.4 (1991): 616-622.
- Moore, R.C. (1959). Arthropoda I - Arthropoda General Features, Proarthropoda, Euarthropoda General Features, Trilobitomorpha. Treatise on Invertebrate Paleontology. Part O. Boulder, Colorado/Lawrence, Kansas: Geological Society of America/University of Kansas Press. ISBN 0-8137-3015-5.
- Phleger Jr, Fred B. "Lichadian trilobites." *Journal of Paleontology* (1936): 593-615.
- R. A. Fortey and A. P. Heward. 2015. A new, morphologically diverse Permian trilobite fauna from Oman. Acta Palaeontologica Polonica 60:201-216
- Shiino, Yuta, et al. "Swimming capability of the remopleuridid trilobite Hypodicranotus

striatus: Hydrodynamic functions of the exoskeleton and the long, forked hypostome." *Journal of theoretical biology* 300 (2012): 29-38.

- Tripp, Ronald Pearson. "The classification and evolution of the superfamily Lichacea (Trilobita)." *Geological Magazine* 94.02 (1957): 104-122.
- Viersen, van, A.P. (2004). "De mythe van Phacops latifrons [The Myth of Phacops latifrons]". Grondboor & Hamer. 3/4: 66–68.
- Walcott, C.D. Middle Cambrian Branchiopoda, Malacostraca, Trilobita, and Merostomata. In: Cambrian Geology and Paleontology II. Smithsonian. 1914
- Walossek, Dieter. *Morphology, ontogeny, and life habit of Agnostus pisiformis from the Upper Cambrian of Sweden*. Oslo: Universitetsforl., 1987.
- Whiteley, Thomas Edward, Gerald J. Kloc, and Carlton Elliot Brett. *Trilobites of New York: an illustrated guide*. Ithaca, NY: Cornell University Press, 2002.
- Whittington, Harry B. "The Corynexochina (Trilobita): a poorly understood suborder." *Journal of Paleontology* 83.1 (2009): 1-8.

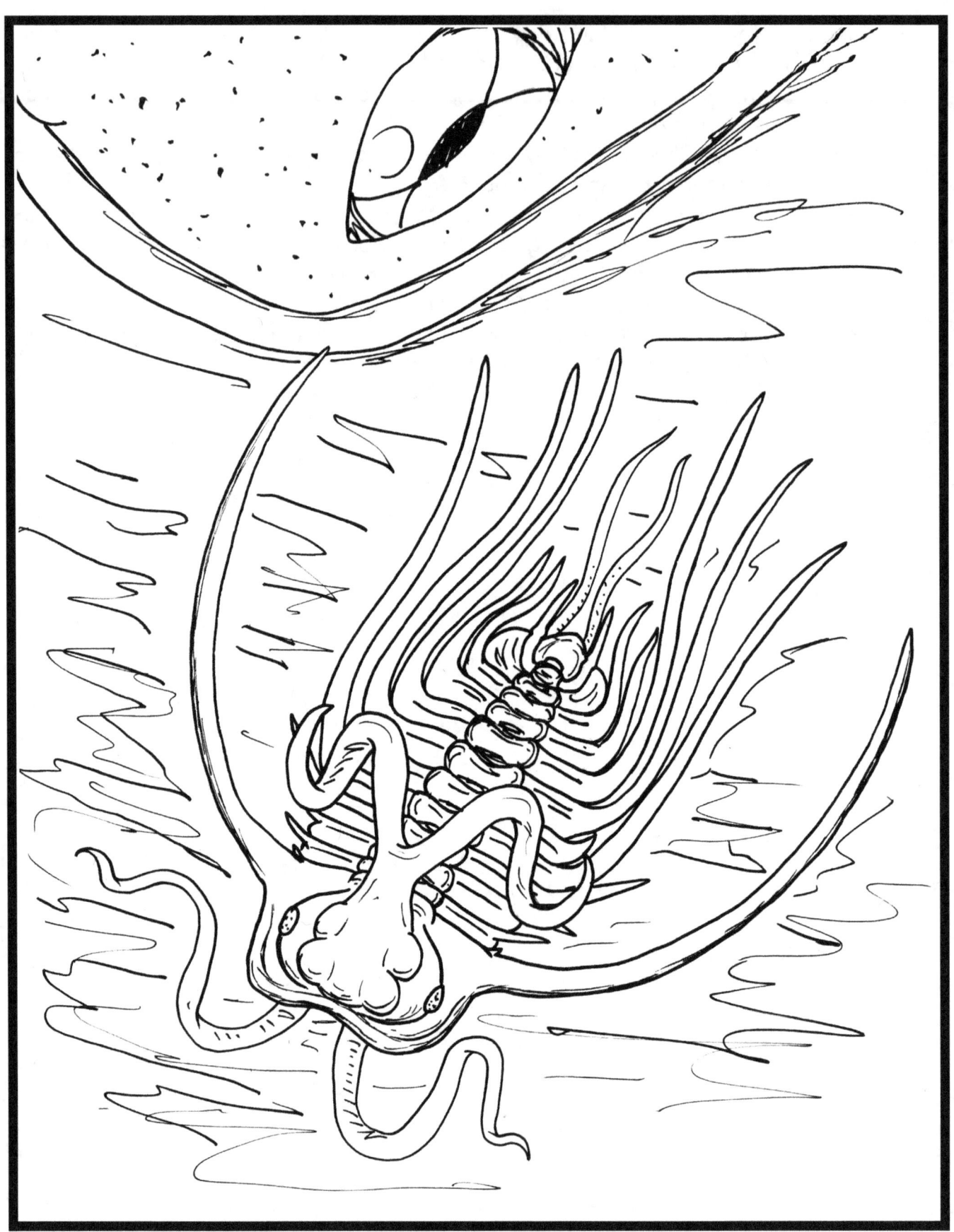

About the Artist

Stanton F. Fink is a student of Biology and Chinese Medicine, and makes a hobby of drawing monsters and researching flowers, arcane-looking creatures, prehistoric animals, fish, reptiles, birds and the occasional, really grotesque fungal fruiting body.

Stanton grew up and went to school in California and is currently living, drawing, and gardening in Oregon.

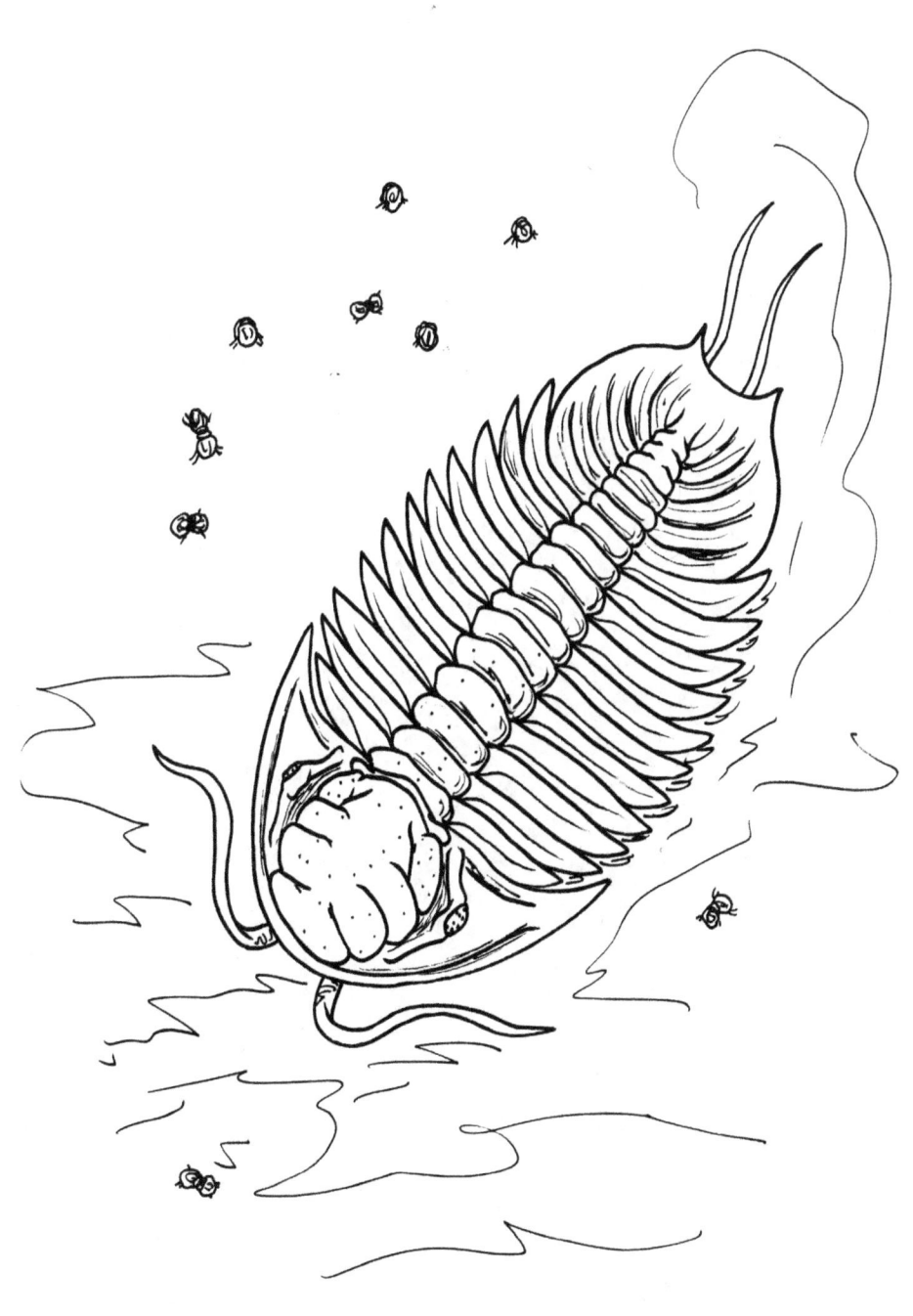